Motivational Workbook

25 Days for Motivating Yourself to Obtain Success

Life is a Marathon. You are in Control of You. You run it ...

Kianna M. Lavender

25 Days for Motivating Yourself to Obtain Success Motivational Workbook

© Copyright 2023 – Kianna M. Lavender

ISBN : 979-8-218-16698-4

For worldwide distribution. Printed in the United States

Kianna M. Lavender

Born and raised in Cleveland Ohio in the inner city. I attended Catholic schools from preschool to graduating 8th grade. Obtained my High school diploma from Jane Addams Business Careers Center. Went off to Cleveland State University then derailed to Columbus where I spent six and a half years attending community college and obtained a Medical Assisting Certification. Realizing that my calling was not in southern Ohio I returned to my roots to begin again. While raising two girls I knew that success was my ultimate determination. Finished college at Tiffin University obtaining a Master of Science concentrating in Homeland Security. None of this was easy. When I think back on it all; being a teen mom, working multiple jobs, attending school, going through the police academy, battling with depression, dealing with stresses of not truly having a solid foundation for what path to take. By the Grace of God was the only reason I can say that I am the Queen Of My Success.

I dedicate this Workbook to all Queens …

Always remember that you are beautiful and never forget that you are "The Queen of Your Success."

You are a Queen because you were born into an extraordinary Kingdom.

QUEEN= *ruler, monarch, powerful,* YOU.

Q   *Qualified*
U   *Unique*
E   *Exceptional*
E   *Extraordinary*
N   *Nirvana*

As a Queen you must know how positively marvelous you are. It is in your natural nature to be seen as royalty. If you had the opportunity to read my book I described how and what I think of when I am outlining a Queen.

In the terms here I am using one word to describe each letter in Queen. These words can be a part of your daily affirmations and ways to manifest you as the Queen you are.

You are Q UALIFIED

You are U NIQUE

You are E XCEPTIONAL

You are E XTRAORDINARY

You are N IRVANA

Qualified = entitled to a particular benefit, profession, desire; being eligible based on your experiences or education; able and ready to conquer anything.

Unique = one of a kind, original, special, eccentric, rare, especial type; nothing you have ever encountered.

Exceptional = something else, none other, peculiar; not something you will find just anywhere.

Extraordinary = remarkable, amazing, astonishing; polished, cut from a different cloth.

Nirvana = bliss, joy, serenity, tranquil harmony; released from any and all past pain, filled with peace, joy and happiness within.

We are all doing our very best to be the best versions of ourselves. Well that is why you purchased this workbook right?

Doing things that can help you be the best version of yourself is easier said than done.

I have heard this saying a million times:

"A habit is formed after Doing something for 21 days straight. It takes 21 days to Develop a habit. If you Do something for 21 days it will come natural."

Each one of these sayings has something in common, Action! The action comes from you making and taking the initiative to do it.

Develop it & Do it.

What I have here are 25 motivational tasks that will help you to form habits to being on your way to obtaining the success you so desire.

We all have our own true definition of what success means to us. Anything that you set forth to do and obtain is gaining success in it.

I want to take you on a 25 day motivational journey to reaching your version of success.

You have to do the work though!

This is your map, but you have to drive...

Buckle up ...

Ok lets go!

DAY 1

Write a Letter to Your Past Self

Doing this will allow you to put pen to paper some of the things that you want to let go of and forgive yourself for so that you can have the space to move forward to successfully getting over your past.

My thoughts ...

DAY 2

Create An Obtainable Goal List With Due Dates

Notice I said "obtainable" do not sike yourself, you can do anything you put your mind too, write it down and get it done.

My thoughts ...

DAY 3

Declutter!

Declutter your space you live in, declutter your contact list, declutter your social media.

You have to do this in order to create space for the new. Weed out the old in order to allow your vision to see clearer. Removing old things and people will do more than you realize to help advance you towards reaching a level of success. I know it is hard, but removing this clutter will help you more than you know you need it!

My thoughts ...

DAY 4

Find and Face Your Fears

What has been holding you back from _______________) Whatever it may be, find it and face it so that you can overcome it and move forward. If you never face what may be the biggest or smallest fear in your life, you cannot get past it to get to the success level that is behind it.

My thoughts ...

DAY 5

Take Inventory of Who's In Your Circle

Look who has been there and who will be there for you when you need them too. Who you give access to you matters when you are trying to become the best version of YOU! Take a look and go back to "decluttering."

My thoughts ...

DAY 6

Create Some Boundaries

I said "SOME" you must set apart a list of boundaries for how you allow people to show up within your space. Setting the boundaries is a huge part of the first step once you have completed decluttering. Maintaining these boundaries will not happen overnight....

My thoughts ...

. . . .

. . . .

. . . .

. . . .

. . . .

. . . .

Ok, Let Us Take a Short Pause Here and Realize Something

Be patient and Trust the Process. Recognize that not everyone will be willing to accept the growth you are doing. Also, not everyone can see the success you are building towards.

If you are into praying or meditating this is a good time to take a break and do that for these tasks that you have started to work on. These things are amplifying your way of living to be the successful royal Queen in the Kingdom. You are doing your due diligence to be the best version of yourself by doing this work on yourself. You should be proud of your progress.

Now lets keep going!

Be Honest with Yourself, Regroup!

We are one full week into this journey to motivating yourself to obtain the levels of success that you wish to achieve. So at this point be honest with yourself and really focus on the first few things we have been working on here. Take the time to do them and really do it. Be honest, raw, and vulnerable with yourself to do the work.

My thoughts ...

Take a Breather – This Marathon Is Just Starting!

By this time you must have shared what you are doing with a significant other or close friend. If not, it may be time to get an Accountability Partner (AP). Reach out to me if at this point you are struggling and need guidance. I may be able to offer some, I am not a professional, but I can speak from my personal experience.

DAY 8

Get Yourself Some "Deep" Affirmations

Key word here is, yes you guessed it, DEEP! Affirmations are great and very important when you are on the road to building a successful life. Affirmations can be many different varieties of words, phrases, poems, or even songs. The list is endless when it comes to what you are using to affirm and manifest for your life.

My thoughts ...

DAY 9

Remind Yourself of Your "Why"

When it comes to the true reason for WHY you want to be successful and WHY you make the decision to get out of bed and do your day to day routine. Think of the WHY and ways that you can improve on them or change them if necessary. The goal is to never give up and to understand that because you are waking up, there is purpose for your life. Understanding your WHY helps you go harder!

My thoughts ...

DAY 10

Forgive & Move On

Do you have things from your past that are haunting memories or that you struggled to let go of ? If you have not forgiven them it is and will forever take a toll on your life. That old past baggage is old news and now is the time for you to forgive it and move on. No, you do not need to make phone calls, set up meetings, nor send any smoke signals up to let them know this. Forgiveness comes and starts within you and ends with you too. Do it, I am speaking from experience, you will feel much better and lighter afterwards.

My thoughts ...

DAY 11

This Is Not a Race, It Is a Marathon

The work you are doing is no competition for you to win at the finish line by the end of the 25th day here. This is a marathon and a continuous journey for your success on levels for achievement until you have to answer to your maker on judgment day. The marathon will continue if you do not quit. If you have not started to eat healthier, this is a perfect time to begin. Building an interior and exterior healthy habit is a part of your marathon too!

My thoughts ...

. . . .

. . . .

. . . .

. . . .

. . . .

DAY 12

List Your Values

What do you truly value in your life? We have things that we do not want to live our life without. Figure out what those things or people are and truly show them what they mean to you. Now some of these values may be physical, some may be actual people. This is your workbook so (judgment free) what you value is not the same as the next person and that is perfectly fine. Treat what you value with the utmost respect and honor necessary.

My thoughts ...

Mid-Point

Yay!! We are mid-way through getting you to the bestest most successful version of yourself. You should be proud of your progress because you did some things that you may have never thought of or that you may have started and not finished until now. Do not put your pen down yet because you still have more to do. It is crucial to keep moving and also to never forget how far you have come. Remember; Marathon, you have what it takes!

DAY 13

Take a Long Look at Yourself In the Mirror

Face the fact that you are you and the work that you are, were, and want to do is what you have to look at and face each day. Take some time to really take a look at yourself in the mirror. I am talking about your full and authentic nakedness. Tell yourself how much you love yourself and how proud you are of you. Don't regret anything about what you are looking back at in this mirror. If you are not able to love and accept what you are looking at then how can anyone else do that. It starts with you. I said something online before; You are someone else's mirror, be a good reflection and give yourself Grace, you deserve it!

My thoughts ...

DAY 14

Self-Care It Up!

When was the last time that you really took some time to dig into some of the things that you love to do. We hear more and more about self-care these days and most of us look past it. Whatever self-care means to you, take this day and do it. If you are clueless on what some things could be, think about what are some things that you do and enjoy and do those. Some of mine are, spa time, rearranging my closet, shopping, watching a good movie, reading and journaling to name a few.

My thoughts ...

Connect with Your AP

Just in case you have not done this when I mentioned it earlier. This is when you really need to dive deep into the things you have been working on and share them with someone that is going to hold you accountable to sticking to them. Your AP can be anyone, but must be someone that you can trust to throw some tough love your way. Your AP can also be a professional mentor, therapist, or counselor. Anyone that can help keep you on track. So, set up the time to meet with them, if you do not set it up today when will it happen?

My thoughts ...

Almost There ... Keep Pushing!

Speaking of track; we have 10 days left! Let's recap here. Now I just mentioned some of the things that I do for my self-care it up time. One of those included journaling. In case you have not looked, there is a section for journaling in this very book. The space to do this may not be enough for you to use forever. Treat yourself to a blank notebook. This notebook does not have to be anything fancy, but make sure that it is something that you can keep up with or use the notes section of your cell phone. Recap what you have done, track your progress.

Let's get ready to keep training for this marathon. To do that, you will need tools. Those tools include you remaining positive that you are not in this alone. Recall what I said about you being a reflection in the mirror to others. You can pour into others as long as your cup is not empty. The work you have done so far has been allowing you to fill up your cup so that you are not drained and can pour back into the world around you. This type of endurance is building your levels of success simultaneously.

DAY 16

Solo Trip It, Take That Trip!

This is something that I never thought I would or could do. I did and so can you. It may feel weird or uncomfortable to do this for some people. But I am telling you, it was a liberating thing once I struck up the courage to do it. Taking a trip alone can really show you and teach you stuff. Stuff about yourself and stuff about the place you choose that you never could do with others. If you are not able to travel that is ok. Start with doing things in a part of town that you may have never done (be smart) choose a safe space. Also, always let someone know where you are, like your AP. Online there are many solo-trip checklists to review also.

My thoughts ...

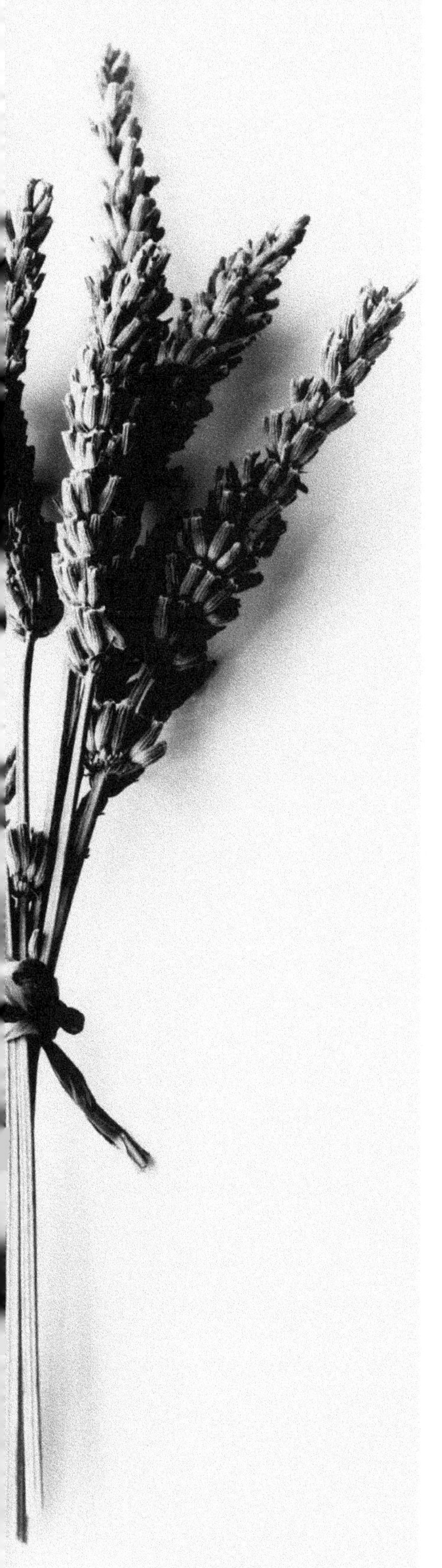

DAY 17

Update Your Resume

You may or may not be in the market for a new position. This is a prime opportunity to see how far you have come or where there is still work to be done professionally. Updating your resume will show you the areas where you may be weak and also your strengths. Resume writing practice is offered online and also at most local libraries. Staying current with this allows you the privilege to be ready just in case. There is not ever a bad time to have a well polished resume. If you stay ready, then you will never have to get ready. This also depends on how you choose to dress for your day. When you are well dressed, you feel good and will show up better in the role you are in. This shows up in your mood, energy, vibe, and elevates your success overall.

My thoughts ...

Listen to Any Good Podcasts Lately?

My Podcast knowledge was zero about 3-4 years ago. People mentioned Podcasts and I turned my nose up because I thought it was silly. Finding out later that so much really good information can come from listening to them. There are so many motivational, funny, informational, story telling, health & fitness, the list goes on and on for the various Podcasts available. Podcast shows are the new age way of entertainment on so many levels. Tune in and find some that can help you on your success journey. A few that I tune into are Affirmations for Black Girls, JD Inspo, The Equation, On Purpose, #Matter, Transformed Empowered Mindset just to name a few. I have a Podcast as well called Spread Your Wings, Queen.

My thoughts ...

. . . .

. . . .

DAY 19

Give Yourself Some Grace

Don't beat yourself up so much, don't be so hard on yourself....these are sayings that we hear when we want to do something and it does not get done, or it is taking a long time to happen. Giving yourself Grace through the process is how you can allow what is supposed to happen, happen. It will do so gracefully if it is meant to be. Anything worth having will take time to develop. My metaphor of the butterfly in my book is just that. You too, my friend, are blooming and growing more and more successful each day. Putting in the work is where it will show up in the end. During the process, give yourself Grace to get there. On this journey here look at the exceptional things you've accomplished.

My thoughts ...

. . . .

. . . .

. . . .

. . . .

DAY 20

Check In with the New Version of You

You have put in some serious work and the progress is showing. How do you feel now, do you need to back track it to Day 3 and clean more things out, or do you need another attempt to do the solo trip? Either way or whatever way the flow of things has happened. There really is not a specific order of how you need to do things. At this stage you have stayed committed to working on yourself and you should be super proud. Always remember to check in with yourself from time to time to recap and focus.

My thoughts ...

DAY 21

Date Night

You have really done well and it is time to celebrate and recognize your growth. Now again, this is no race so you did not win yet. Taking time to celebrate progress is equally important. What better way to celebrate is to get all dressed up and look as good on the outside as you are feeling on the inside! Now, where to go you ask. Well you do not have to officially leave your home if you are not up to it or like crowds. You can set the date mood anywhere you see fit. Feel free to invite your significant other or your AP if you wish. But this is celebrating your time because you deserve it!

My thoughts ...

. . . .

. . . .

. . . .

. . . .

DAY 22

What Is on Your Playlist

If you do not already have an official mood lifting motivational song or play list it is time to get one. Music for me is really special as I mentioned in my first book. Music does something to me and it really helps to settle your mood. Motivational music can and will be different for everyone. Find the tunes that work for you and try to play them at least once a day from here on out. These songs are to help you, move you, grow you, motivate you, empower you, and to keep you running smoothly through your marathon.

My thoughts ...

The Number 22

This is one of the double digit angel numbers, if you are not familiar, google it "Angel Numbers"... I just got into them a few years ago and they help ground me whenever I notice them in my presence. This number and a few others 111, 22, 44, 55 to name a few.

DAY 23

Stop and Smell the Flowers

When was the last time you bought flowers for yourself? This gesture is one of the smallest ways to do something kind and thoughtful for yourself. Pouring into yourself is very important. Taking time to do small things helps encourage you to do this for not only yourself but for others as well. No special occasion has to be the reason, just because flowers means a lot. Don't' like flowers, try balloons, or a nice candle. The gesture goes a long way.

My thoughts ...

DAY 24

Have You Prayed?

When was the last time that you really sat down or got on your knees, closed your eyes, collapsed your hands and really prayed? I am guilty for not doing prayer like this as often as I should. He is listening regardless but having the specific time and space to really spend time with your God is crucial to your success. We tend to forget some of the things that we prayed for and once we get them we forget to thank and continue our prayers. Prayer is very similar to meditation and can be done in any method that you feel is necessary.

My thoughts ...

Don't Repeat the Cycle, But Repeat It

You are new! You are born again, you have accomplished what you started and have finished what you never knew was at stake. There are many cycles in our life, some that need to be repeated, tweaked, changed and some that never need to see the light of day ever again. This marathon to your success is a cycle that you must fight for daily and never give up on it. Reward your wins, big or small. Record your losses because if you never fail that means you never tried. All of what you did may have been uncomfortable. You must remember that you should get comfortable being uncomfortable because any new thing will never be familiar to you. You have created some new healthy habits....

My thoughts ...

. . . .

. . . .

What's next?

You are in charge of what happens next....

Congratulations for completing these 25 days in motivating yourself!!

Please use this space to journal and keep track of success ... Let the marathon go on and on and how you navigate it is all up to YOU!

Please stay connected with me:

Website: queenofmysuccess.org

Instagram: iamthe_queenofmysuccess.org

Podcast: Spread Your Wings Queen

Email: Queensuccess25@gmail.com

I would love to hear about your 25 day motivational journey!